RIVER CITY FIRES
DEREK ANNIS

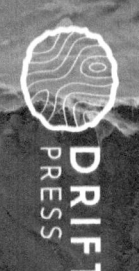

Independently published by *Driftwood Press*
in the United States of America.

Managing Poetry Editor: Jerrod Schwarz
Editor: Andrew Hemmert
Guest Judge: Carl Phillips
Front & Back Cover Image: Adam Hall
Cover Design: Sally Franckowiak & Jerrod Schwarz
Innards Design & Copyeditor: James McNulty
Fonts: Rift Soft, Cinzel, Garamond, & Merriweather

Copyright © 2023 by Derek Annis
All Rights Reserved.

No part of this publication
may be reproduced, stored in a retrieval
program, or transmitted, in any form or by
any means (electronic, mechanical,
photographic, recording, etc.), without
the publisher's written permission.

First published on December 12th, 2023
ISBN-13: 978-1-949065-29-9

Please visit our website at www.driftwoodpress.com
or email us at editor@driftwoodpress.net.

PRAISE FOR
RIVER CITY FIRES

"To make of bewilderment itself a world serviceable enough to live in—to imagine a way through: this seems the chief imperative of *River City Fires*, whose astonishing poems hover around fires both actual and metaphorical in a landscape/riverscape/forestscape both recognizable and surreal. These are poems whose meanings I can't always parse—and I don't feel I'm supposed to; instead, they seem like slant confessions, not of trauma, but from trauma; they articulate the triumph of survival, they fragment what's whole and, instead of restoring it, reimagine the possibilities for wholeness. 'Blessed are the burned. The blistered/ inherit the earth.' A terrific collection."

—Carl Phillips,
winner of the Pulitzer Prize for Poetry

"*River City Fires* is beautiful, elemental, and oracular. It's as steeped in threat as any fable or holy book, and the darkness is forever manifesting into fears and friends. Like the book of Proverbs armed with a rifle, every poem transforms themselves at each line break's dire revelations. Surreal and archetypal, this city and its fires speak (as many fires do) to god, asking 'make death/turn away.' These poems will haunt you with the most gorgeous aching."

—Traci Brimhall,
author of *our lady of the ruins*

"Derek Annis' poems reveal that the space between the mythic & the mundane is more like a folded up map than a border, that in these lives of ours, which grow evermore unparsable with each day, the most surreal & uncontainable thing is a real & true emotion."

—Mathias Svalina,
author of *The Wine-Dark Sea*

"The survivor speaker of Derek Annis' *River City Fires* emerges as if from a smoldering landfill, backlit with the explosions of an unmistakable apocalypse. Everything here is creature and born of a warped world that has shaped its inhabitants in its own reflection. Which is why it feels strange to say the poems here are often very funny, as sad as they are. It's as if each poem carries inside it a piece of flint which Anis' stark and abrupt language inevitably strikes into flame. In this book, you will find words never before paired to create worlds never before imagined that are scary, wonderful, horrible, and undeniable. This chapbook book is a wonderful, bloody machine."

—Cate Marvin,
author of *Oracle*

CONTENTS

Weapon	1
Manifest	7
Skin	8
Excision	9
Potato Salad	10
Still Life with Razor Blades	11
Social Phobia	12
Aviary	13
Damages	14
Independence Day	15
At the Church of Blue Light	16
Holy City	17
Dysgeusia	19
Light Work	20
Descent	21
After the Funeral	22
Pitch	23
Sunk	24
The Feeding	25
Night Watch	26
Hundred Year Summer	28
Domestic	29
Lullaby	33
Agency	34
Interview	37

WEAPON

It was the stick
I loved
the cave
the wolves
carried me
scared boy
one humid afternoon

I came to rest
with shining
fractured rib
broken teeth
the world
a needle
the tongue reckless
under the needle

I'm small
machine boy
automatic weapon
I've been the dust
a shadow
the mouth
of another

nails
pulled teeth
wind and scraps
of metal
a gallon
of earth
a skull
in the water

I discover
the hollow god
blood in my glass

I split and curl
spit smoke
call me a faint
memory of losing
I plant nails
with salt
or ash
of tongue
a sharp stick
a mouth
a wet skull

this town
a fire
the sky
missing
my fix
hypodermic
a septic water

house of feathers
gathers noise

I seal
the door
can live
a year
sleeping

god
make death

turn away

MANIFEST

The fathers forced open the mouth of the forest, made it shout a city across the valley. An orchestra of sparks and shining steel frightened the sky, which waited for nightfall and snuck to the hills. Great storms of birds flew into the fields reflected on picture windows, clapped against the asphalt with bone-pierced throats. The people of the city took up shovels, went back to the forest and extracted a wealth of symbols, which they organized according to brightness. The symbols were cold. For fear of the dark, the city kept its eyes open at all times. The dark receded into the trees. The orchestra played through the night.

SKIN

I was a boy with curly
brown hair. I had
all my skin. I wore it
under the stars
like a white dress.
I went to the field to lie
in the tall grass. I carried a jar
of eyes. Wet noise
against glass. The fire
was miles away.
I lay in the field
with all my skin. Specks of ash
fell from the sky. A film
on my hair, my tongue.
I held the jar of eyes
like an infant, lifted
its mouth to my breast. Wet
noise. After a time, the eyes grew
teeth. Bright noise
of breaking glass. I could hear
the fire grow
close. I lay
in the tall grass. The eyes
bit into my skin
like ticks: green
and brown and full
of blood. Glass like
diamonds in my skin.
Ash fell from the sky.

EXCISION

Father had anvils for hands. Solid lead retinas. Fingers growing out of his throat. He stuck his buckshot tongue to a fir tree in the shady back acre of our property. Magpies still come by to shake the salt from it, use its shine to sharpen their little knives. Father could taste a storm from a mile away. He could strike sparks from ivy vines and set fire loose on the town like a pack of wild hogs. He drank whisky straight from the barrel of his rifle. He let his big voice undress atop the table and piss in everyone's drinks. He never married. He could bury anybody. They say he's still out there, somewhere, stuffing his ears with hornets and cutting the bones from his feet.

POTATO SALAD

Growing up, the best part of summer
was the family picnic
in the public park, and the best part
of the family picnic was the appearance
of uncle frank, who chewed
the wet butts of cheap cigars
and wore prosthetic earlobes
where his eyelids
used to be. Each year,
he let us kids pick our favorite
dried leaf from his breast.
There were many leaves.
The selection process
took many hours.
Since I was the luckiest
of the kids, I always picked
the leaf with the most
ticks. The others scowled at me
in a display of profound
reverence. Uncle frank and I
had a laugh at their expense,
and observed the family tradition
of bashing them with sticks.
Then, just as suddenly as he appeared
uncle frank was off again,
into the lake, waving goodbye
with his stone hands. *Goodbye,*
uncle frank! we said. *Goodbye, frank!*
said the thousands of spiders
gliding gracefully down
from pine boughs overhead.

STILL LIFE WITH RAZOR BLADES

Matt imagined a fishing line and cast it into the yard. He wore a cedar bark suit and I gave him the last of my eggs wrapped in a feather boa. *Here* I said *these are the last of my eggs.* Matt mixed turpentine with whisky and dipped his bad eye in it. We could tell it worked because the eye went lilac and lit up like a pinball machine. I had the only fingers on the block. Everyone wanted a pair. People wearing hats rode by on the backs of great magpies saying *beautiful weather today neighbor* and *the mouth of the mine has widened.* Soon it will consume the earth. When night cut evening's throat to let the dark out Matt and I sat on the patio under the whiteblue floodlight. All around us the fish jumped. I smoked so much my teeth turned raisin and fell out of my mouth. In their porcelain bowl the razor blades looked sweet as pears.

SOCIAL PHOBIA

I made a new friend
from scraps
of dark I found
in the alleys
of my city

stitched him together
with silver thread
draped him over
a skeletal system
of sticks

I said *I am a cube of sugar*
in a glass of ice

when he placed his hands
on my shoulders
I could see his eyes
were missing

when he tried to speak
ribbons of skin
fell from his mouth

AVIARY

I eat all the waffles I can stuff
into my father's boots.
I have an electric cinderblock
for the collection plate.
I shut the waterfall
off and ride my horse
to dust. Police officers
shake their fingers
all the way to the bank
of the river, where no car tires
trade cigarettes for laughs.
In the laps of their giant mothers,
cigar smoking robots click
into gear and fire
the gravedigger.
He has mouths to feed
to the pigs. Enough
for another month
or two, during which time
he can apply
to himself
a second coat
of gold paint
and hide in the basement
of my paper house
where blackbirds splash
against the walls
like bags of nails.

DAMAGES

Asphalt exhaled waves of heat as I drove out beyond the city limit, onto a road of dust. A suffocating cloud emerged from under my wheels. I pulled to the side, began speaking to a vast congregation of wildflowers. *I bring news from the city,* I said, *we have rerouted the river to pass through our homes, where we will use it to carry our waste to the sea.* I gestured to a dry creek bed, which was beginning to crack at the edge of the meadow. The flowers bowed their heads in waves of sorrow, dropped their seeds on the dry earth. *Do not despair,* I urged them, *the mayor has signed a resolution into law; each of you will receive a voucher for one free makeover.* An elderberry bush in the back row collapsed; a plume of dust rose, dissolved on the wind like a spirit. *The horses at Clover Stables received makeovers last week,* I assured them, *and I'm happy to tell you they look like stars when the moon lights their bones.* I removed a rubber band from around the vouchers, which were printed on squares of gray paper, and placed one at the foot of each flower.

INDEPENDENCE DAY

The dog lies in cool grass
and chews her scrap of hide.
Fireworks shimmer
your fingers away
forever. Watch them
squirm in the dirt like worms
regurgitated from a robin's
eye socket. A sky
red as your childhood
lake, descends like autumn's
last apple; the sound of gravity
stuck in its own raw throat.
Your head swells like seared
corn seed. The dog hacks up
her scrap of hide, snaps
her braided tail like a whip.
From atop their towers of salt,
blonde children sing
bullets into existence. Pay the fee
or suffer a season of embers.
You're in god's mouth now.

AT THE CHURCH OF BLUE LIGHT

In place of wafers, preacher
places blue taffy on your tongue.
To receive it, kneel, open
mouthed, inside the dome
of blue light before the altar.

If upon you preacher
places hands, it means
he sees within you
something he likes
to eat. Cover
your neck. Press
your knees against
your chest to protect
the organ meats.
Fear not; his gnawing

will stop
when the organist
treats the congregation
to a composition
of gnashing teeth.
The parishioners will join
hands and gnash along.

As the service comes to a close,
a candle is passed
around the room. The wax runs.
Blessed are the burned. The blistered
inherit the earth.

HOLY CITY

a crowd gathers
atop the slaughterhouse
to watch the rocket
propelled frog finger
a feather bath

dogs spoon around
my basement eating
the peanut butter
chandeliers

and a shoal
of molten glass

rolls off my tongue
like an afternoon
credit card

no more geese in the river
of carpet remnants

no more pie for the queen
her wet tentacles
suck the wheel
of fortune and spin
snakes into the earth
like a hydraulic drill

the surgeon drops a stitch
and steps outside
for a breath of fresh syrup

while a tiger prepares to strike
sparks from the foreskin
of the golden calf

we all want
what jesus wants: thin-sliced
kittens with a side
of unleavened
lead-poisoned adolescents

here he comes now
for a second time
with rifle and knife
ready to collect

DYSGEUSIA

The city's encircled by fire.
The ants are buzzing.
I've acquired a rifle from the honeymaker's son,
who's late to the wedding
again. Every time mother washes her hair
down the drain, a plate of figs appears
on my ottoman. They're sweet as children
in a river of mud
with their mouths open wide like baby birds
on an autopsy table. Little fluorescent ribs
smoke like a notion of home. I was there once,
in the retina of a mouse, helpless
as a horse on springs, dead man's face
on the pillow next to mine.
Nothing will ever taste as good as that.
I've run out of ice. My spoons
are losing blood.

LIGHT WORK

My four decorative typewriters
on the turntable pump out
a mouth of bees every three hours
Sheila hates them
and beats them
with a blown-out robin's beak
and when she's done she dances
the horseshoe around town
picking rosaries
from beneath her fingernails
where marionettes gather wind
and wait for tanks
to sing munitions

meanwhile
in the cellar
a sore throat scratches
notes in the lightbulbs
so the dark
will have something to read

DESCENT

I'm on a fully booked flight from Texas to Earth. The passenger next to me, a priest with crucifix burns on his face, was hired by the airline to maintain the safety of the plane through the power of prayer. He separates woodpeckers from their wings and discards the latter into the aisle. His carry-on is full of woodpeckers. The pile of wings is knee-high. I ask him to stop, as the woodpecker dander aggravates my hanging eardrum, which is already swollen with altitude. Undeterred, he draws a red pentagram on the air between us, mumbles a catholic spell in Latin, and continues his work. My hanging eardrum, instantly healed, turns white as a baby's bones. In a fit of turbulence, the plane shakes free of its wings, born again as a bomb.

AFTER THE FUNERAL

I stuffed my pockets
with rose stems
and went grocery shopping

I was chewing screws
and spitting blood

all around me
the other shoppers
squeezed tomatoes
and avocadoes

a whole family
of rats burrowed
into my throat

a voice from the ether
requested a second checker

PITCH

Thin men walked the trails in their formal gowns. They moved like water between enormous granite formations, licked thumbs and made champagne flutes sing. The singing carried itself out of the valley and fell upon the people of the city like the sweet smoke of autumn sage. Sweet smoke of song carried the people of the city into sleep. Thin men walked the trails in their formal gowns. River through the rocks. The people of the city slept in rooms of falsetto smoke so sweet it made the children weep.

SUNK

I live at the river's edge
where the eyes open
their mouths and tongue
each other blind
my neighbor has mud
on his legs and his head
is wet leather
he loves to mow his lawn
he loves to feed birds
to the mower

my floorboards swell
and split with heat
I have a knife
on my hip
a shotgun
tongue

the infants
in the river
never cry

their little boats
are made of gold

THE FEEDING

A dog trotted out of the woods and laid
its tongue at my feet. I slapped it
against my upper thigh
to test for wetness. It was dry
as an old sock. We took it to the vet
under the freeway. He took one
look at it and spat
up a scalpel. *Do it yourself*, he said.
I picked up the scalpel. It went straight
through my palm.
Great, said the vet,
now he thinks he's jesus.
Noticing that I was jesus, parishioners gathered.
Check this out, I commanded.
I sliced the tongue down the center.
It became two tongues.
I sliced those two tongues down the center,
and they became four.
I sliced those four, and so on,
until I had 5,000 and was able to feed
everyone in attendance.
They could hardly believe it.

NIGHT WATCH

In the slim hour of forest
where Rick lives
stands a little house
long abandoned
but for the mice
who have chewed
the particle-board floors
straight through
Rick says he left
his car parked
on the second story
we look in every corner
behind every hammer-cracked
continent of sheetrock
and find nothing
but Rick gets real focused
after a long night digging
through the powders
in his dresser drawer
Rick I say *I don't believe*
your car was ever here
to begin with
but he persists
and shakes his jar
of bottle caps in my face
and no matter how I insist
that *those aren't keys*
and they sure as hell won't
start your car
Rick keeps drilling
at the foundation

looking under every scrap
of dried mouse and spitting
chunks of bitten cheek on the floor
like sunflower seeds
I'm exhausted and I want
to go home but
I'm pretty fond of Rick
so I stick around all night
and listen for headlights
just in case

HUNDRED-YEAR SUMMER

we went for a drive
in the country
the car was on fire

we left a black wake of smoke
on a sea of trees
a red eye rose

from the deep
noise we dumped
into the river

we parked in the mud
beside a dead barn
the barn was on fire

inside we found a baby
starling dying in a nest
of dead starlings

the nest was on fire
smoke leaked through
the barn's soft roof

we lit our cigarettes
red eyes floated
in the smoke the eyes were

on fire somebody said *drink*
and we drank somebody said
load the pipe and lit a fire

smoke-red eye rose
over the river the river
burned

DOMESTIC

It was 96 degrees
in the house. You bashed
your fists against
a ball of bread dough.

You wore jean shorts
and a sleeveless
floral-print shirt. Steam
rose from a pot
on the stove. I was
lying on the couch
sipping scotch,
watching faces emerge
from the ceiling.

You had sweat
on your forehead.
Your tattoos
were all wet.

We were in love.
I was lying
on the couch
with my mouth
full of sand.
Someone split me
open, left
an ant hill in place
of my lungs.

We went to bed.
It was 103 degrees.
A box fan
raked embers of air
over our naked bodies.
You told me
not to worry.
You said: *no one
can tell there's a hill
of ants inside. Your face
is blank.*

I said: *I want
to empty myself
onto the floor.
There's a hot stone
in my skull; someone poured
water on it.* Our bed
was stuck in the room
like a bent nail. We kissed.
My tongue
bit your tongue.
You slicked
your hair back
with blood.

The house was quiet
as a dead cat.
In our sleep,
we took each other
apart, leaving limbs
on the floor.

When we woke,
we found two
blonde daughters
toddling around
the room.
They picked up
our pieces and began
stitching us back together

with their clumsy
little fingers. They sewed
my ears to your cheek,
stitched your head
to the bottom
of my foot. They squealed
with delight while
squishing eyeballs
between their toes.

You smiled
wide, said:
*Oh, I love
their tiny voices!*

Yes, I said,
*and the way they hold
my forefingers
in their little hands.*

*How they stumble
through the room,*
you said, *like drunks.*

*We are the luckiest
couple alive,* we agreed.

When the daughters
tired of sewing,
they took turns nursing
at a breast they had taken
to bed.

LULLABY

I was smoking
in the attic. You entered

and untied my face.
Downstairs, our children
cried in cradles
of ice.

You took off
your earrings
and your fingernails
and lined them neatly

on the desk. I stubbed
my cigarette and lit another
mouse on fire.

Heavy with snow
the house buckled.

You took off your coat
and your feet
and hung them

on hooks. You held me
to you chest
and sang.

Our children cried
beads of ice.

AGENCY

I'm out on a little mountain lake. The mountains are covered in snow. A border of ice grows between the shore and my yellow canoe. I row. My oars make no ripples. My canoe does not move.

The blue children of the lake take turns wearing a pair of wings, which they ripped from a living duck. They splash around, flap the wings wildly while saying, *look at me, mother. I'm flying. I'm on my way to the sea.*

The front of my canoe points true north. No ripples. It will not move. The wingless duck swims circles. Her wake throws flashes of light in all directions, disrupting reflected sky. *Stop taunting me*, I say. My canoe refuses to cut across the water.

The blue children of the lake lock arms, forming a long line. The one in the center flaps wings and takes flight, pulling the others behind in a great V. In the gray flesh of the sky, a gash opens. The blue children slip into it, calling, *we're flying, mother. We're on our way to the sea.*

INVITE THEM INSIDE
A CONVERSATION WITH DEREK ANNIS & JERROD SCHWARZ

First, I wanted to say that it's been a joy to publish *River City Fires*! This is a stunning chapbook, and I can't wait to discuss your inspirations and craft. Let's start with one of the collection's most noticeable facets: the stunning language. These poems move entropically through metaphor, time, geography, and perspective, but they are scaffolded with phenomenal word choice and genuinely striking syntax. What does your writing process look like? How do these poems evolve from the first draft (or first thought) to the final version?

Thank you for your kind words, Jerrod. It's been wonderful working with you, and I'm excited to see my work published by such a great press.

I think I get the best results when I take an organic approach to composing poems. When I sit down to write, I try to get entirely out of the poem's way. I want it to feel like I'm following the poem wherever it happens to go. I want it to feel less like I'm writing a poem, and more like I'm documenting its movements. For me, this approach leads to a more surprising and enjoyable experience of writing. When I start feeling like I have to convey some predetermined message, like I have to make sense, or like I have to keep the poem from wandering beyond arbitrary formal or conceptual boundaries, I know it's time to take a break.

Sometimes my poems invite me into a memory. These poems lead me through the landscape of that memory and, if it goes well, show me previously undiscovered connecting pathways to places beyond its borders. The poems in *River City Fires* are the result of a different approach. I didn't start them with any particular memory or image in mind. Without any memories to follow or predetermined details to include, these poems find their way by following sound. The first sentence of "Still Life with Razor Blades" is a good example: "Matt imagined a fishing line and cast it into the yard." If that sentence had started with a name other than

Matt, it likely wouldn't have included the words "imagined," "cast," or "yard." If the first word had been different, the poem would have taken an entirely different direction. The same is true, I think, for all the poems in *River City Fires*.

I love the onus of these poems: a beginning that is not rooted in memory. It's interesting that you connect this to sound. What kinds of sounds are you drawn to in poetry? Perhaps more specifically, what place does rhythm have in your work?

I'm really drawn to assonance and consonance. I think those two sonic devices contribute a lot to a poem's tone, and they seem to happen naturally when I'm writing. I often use assonance and consonance to guide the revision process, too. If a line or sentence isn't onomatopoeic, that is, if its sounds don't meet with its content in a way that creates resonance, then it's worth examining whether those sounds are making a useful contribution to the poem. In some cases, a contradiction between sound and content can add tension and tonal complexity to a poem, in which case those lines can stay. In other cases, such a contradiction causes tonal confusion, and the lines need to be cut.

I don't pay much attention to rhythm when I'm writing a first draft, but patterns tend to develop anyway. These patterns are most apparent at the points where they shift or break, so those points require special attention during revision. Rhythm has a significant impact on a poem's momentum. If one of my poems makes a big conceptual leap, then it's necessary for the poem to gather enough speed to make that leap and land smoothly on the other side. A shift in rhythm is one way to supply the poem with that speed.

These poems feel abstract but intentional; I can sense a kinship with the avantgarde work of Zachary Schomburg or Tomaž Šalamun. I would love to know your thoughts on lyric poetry. What do you think nonlinear and nonnarrative poetry can say that other genres (or even other art forms in general) might not be able to?

A successful lyric poem is one that transfers, not just conveys, an emotional state or experience from the poet to the reader. Linear narratives and realism can also accomplish this, but not for every kind of experience. I think it's often the case that traumatic or ecstatic experiences are particularly difficult to transfer by using facts or details rooted in realism. The facts of a traumatic event can certainly evoke an emotional response in readers, most often pity, but they fail to transfer the emotional experience of those events. There's an unnamable heaviness to such an experience, an unreality of navigating the world in the midst of it, a disorientation caused by it, a sense that you have been violently separated from yourself, and a sense that the external world has changed—its laws suspended—as a result of your internal experience. I think lyric poetry is a more effective way to transfer such experiences, and that including the facts of those experiences can hinder that effort. With realism and narrative, readers are often looking in from the outside. Lyric poems invite them inside.

These are wonderful insights! They echo what Gregory Orr once said about the lyric poem, that it "extends its survival efficacy outward toward those listeners or readers who respond to the poem's situation as if it were, in some way, their own." What thoughts do you have on your audience's relationship to lyric poems? More broadly, does the audience play any part in your writing?

I make a deliberate effort to forget about the audience when I'm writing. I'm a pretty self-conscious person. I worry about being disliked, I worry about being misunderstood, I'm easily embarrassed, and I have a bad case of imposter syndrome. If I were to consider the audience, all that self-doubt and anxiety would prevent me from writing anything honest, and there are few things less compelling than dishonest poetry. In other words, considering the audience would reduce the likelihood that they connect with my poems in any meaningful way.

That being said, I can generally tell how the audience is likely to react to reading my poems based on how I reacted to writing them. If the poem didn't surprise me when I wrote it, it's unlikely to surprise anybody who reads it. If I didn't discover something about myself or the world while writing it, then nobody is likely to make any discoveries while reading it. I think my poems are most successful when the experience of reading them mirrors the experience of writing them.

One of the most common questions we get in our inbox from writers is, *what is a chapbook*? While there are very rote definitions determined by page count and publishing limitations, I'm much more interested in the *emotional* reasons for writing a small collection. What were your personal reasons for writing a chapbook?

Well, I can't provide a reason for writing a chapbook because I never intended to write a chapbook. Instead of starting with the intention of writing either a chapbook or full-length collection, I went back through my drafts and searched for connections between poems. The connection between the poems in *River City Fires* that I noticed first was tone, so I put all of my poems with tonal connections into a folder. Next, I noticed that some of those poems had similar details or images, so I put those poems together. When I began placing them next to each other, a story began to emerge, and as that story emerged it developed a chronology. I was then able to use that chronology as an organizing principle. This resulted in a chapbook-length collection of poems. If I had found more poems with a tonal connection when I was going through my drafts, I might have ended up with a full-length collection. My approach to compiling a collection is the same as my approach to writing; I let the poems lead the way.

What is next for Derek Annis? What poetry (or other artform) are you working toward?

Right now, I'm slowly plugging away at a second full-length collection. I have a big pile of drafts, probably around one-hundred poems, that I need to cut down and chip away at to see if it starts to take the shape of a collection. I'm not in a big hurry. My primary goal is to continue enjoying the process of creating, and my secondary goal is to have a manuscript ready to submit in about two years.

It's an obligatory interview question, but always an interesting one for readers: what are some of your favorite poetry collections? Perhaps more specifically, were there any pieces of media that directly influenced this chapbook?

The favorite collections question is a difficult one. If you ask me on another day, I'll have a different answer. That being said, Laura Kasischke's *Space, in Chains* is always the first thing that comes to mind. I've read it a dozen times, and it surprises me every time. Other favorites include Christopher Howell's *Love's Last Number*, Tracy K. Smith's *Life on Mars*, Daniel Borzutzky's *The Performance of Becoming Human*, Ai's *Killing Floor*, Russell Edson's *The Tunnel: Selected Poems*, Laura Read's *Instructions for My Mother's Funeral*, and Heikki Huotari's *The Knowable Emotions*. There are many more, but it would take a month to list them. All of these collections influenced *River City Fires* in one way or another.

What is one piece of writing advice you wish someone had told you earlier in your writing life?

Don't worry about whether the poem you are writing makes sense or conveys meaning. I was really concerned about those things when I first started, and it hindered my ability to experiment and discover. I have found that it's much more gratifying to discover a poem's meaning instead of imposing meaning on it or forcing it to say something it doesn't want to say. Poems thrive when they're allowed to lead. They suffer when they're forced to follow.

THANKS & ACKNOWLEDGEMENTS

I would like to thank Cassandra Bruner, MaryLeauna Christensen, Eli Dunham, Sam Foley, Vladislav Frederick, Christopher Howell, Philip Shaw, Dave Storment, and Taylor Waring for their help and guidance with these poems. Many thanks, too, to Jerrod Schwarz, James McNulty, and the rest of the *Driftwood Press* team for selecting this manuscript as a finalist for the Adrift Chapbook Prize, and to Carl Philips for selecting it as the winner.

I would also like to thank the editors of the following journals, in which some of the poems in this collection originally appeared:

"Damages" and "Manifest" *The Account*, 2017
"Excision" and "Dysgeusia" *Bear Review*, 2022
"Agency" *Bitter Oleander*, 2022
"Still Life with Razor Blades" *Blood Orange Review*, 2023
"Skin" *Epiphany*, 2019
"Pitch" *Michigan Quarterly Review*, 2023
"Potato Salad" *Phantom Drift*, 2020
"At the Church of Blue Light" and "Night Watch" *Quarter After Eight*, 2021

Photography Credit: Dean Davis

Derek Annis (they/he) is a neurodivergent poet from the Inland Northwest. He is the author of *Neighborhood of Gray Houses* (*Lost Horse Press*) and an editor for *Lynx House Press*. Their poems have appeared in *The Account, Colorado Review, Epiphany, The Gettysburg Review, The Missouri Review Online, Spillway, Third Coast*, and many other journals.

OTHER DRIFTWOOD PRESS TITLES

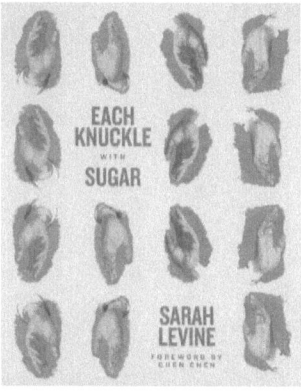

www.ingramcontent.com/pod-product-compliance
Lightning Source LLC
Chambersburg PA
CBHW030140100526
44592CB00011B/975